This book belongs to

_____

...a woman who walks with God.

GROWTH AND STUDY GUIDE

A

Woman's Walk
WITH
GOD

Elizabeth George

HARVEST HOUSE PUBLISHERS
Eugene, Oregon 97402

Cover by Koechel Peterson & Associates, Inc., Minneapolis, Minnesota

A WOMAN'S WALK WITH GOD GROWTH AND STUDY GUIDE
Copyright © 2001 by Elizabeth George
Published by Harvest House Publishers
Eugene, Oregon 97402

ISBN 0-7369-0727-0

Printed in the United States of America.

03 04 05 06 07 08 09 / BP-MS / 10 9 8 7 6 5 4

Acknowledgment

As always, thank you to my dear husband, Jim George, M.Div., Th.M., for your able assistance, guidance, suggestions, and loving encouragement on this project.

Contents

1
Preparing for Greater Growth

Begin this lesson by reading the chapter in your book, *A Woman's Walk with God,* that's titled "Preparing for Greater Growth." Note here any new truths or challenges that stand out to you.

Now that the truths of this chapter are fresh in your mind, recall an occasion when a thriving fruit tree or flowering plant caught your attention.

–Describe the tree or plant.

–What were your thoughts or impressions as you gazed at its glory?

–What do you think contributed to the abundance of its fruit or blooms?

Understanding the Fruit of the Spirit

What can we learn about fruit-bearing from Matthew 7:16-20?

What kind of fruit does Paul speak of in Philippians 1:11?

Write out the nine gracious habits that the Holy Spirit produces in the Christian, found in Galatians 5:22-23. Then learn more about fruit and fruit-bearing from the statements below.

1.

2.

3.

4.

5.

6.

7.

8.

9.

In the New Testament such things as praise of the Lord (Hebrews 13:15), winning converts to Christ (1 Corinthians 16:15), and godly work in general (Colossians 1:10) are spoken of as spiritual fruit produced through believers. But such *action fruit* must come from *attitude fruit*, and that is the kind of fruit Paul focuses on in Galatians 5:22-23. If those *attitudes* are characteristic of a believer's life, the fruit of *active* good works will inevitably follow (emphases added).[1]

Understanding the Problems

There are, as this section of your book pointed out, several "stumbling stones" that we encounter along the path to fruitfulness.

Legalism was mentioned first.

–How was legalism defined?

–What does 1 Corinthians 4:6 say happens when our man-made rules exceed what is written in Scripture?

–What solution does Galatians 5:16 offer?

–And Galatians 5:25?

The flesh is also a problem when it comes to bearing spiritual fruit.

—What do you learn from Galatians 5:17 about the conflict between the flesh and the Spirit?

—And what is the result of fleshly pursuits, according to Galatians 5:19?

—It's an awful thing to have to think about, but go ahead and make a list of the sins and vices in your life.

In the Bible's Song of Solomon, there is a warning about "the little foxes that spoil the vines" (Song of Solomon 2:15). Hear what a Bible teacher of old considers to be some of "the little foxes" that can "spoil" the fruit-bearing process in our walk with God:

Selfishness spoils love.

Discontent spoils joy.

Anxious thought spoils peace.

Impatience spoils patience.

Bitter words spoil kindness.

Indolence spoils goodness.

Doubt spoils faith.

Pride spoils gentleness.

Love of pleasure spoils self-control.[2]

Understanding the Call to "Walk by the Spirit"

What solution to the conflict between the flesh and the Spirit does the inspired pen of Paul give us in Galatians 5:16?

As I tried to define what walking by the Spirit means, I wrote these words:

> In simple terms, walking by the Spirit means living each moment in submission to God. Walking by the Spirit means seeking to please Him with the thoughts we choose to think, the words we choose to say, and the actions we choose to take. And walking by the Spirit means letting Him guide us each step of the way. It's letting Him work within us so that we can bring glory to God (page 14).

Understanding "Abiding in Christ"

Read John 15:1-8. Abiding in Christ is another calling from God that enables us to bear His fruit in our life. What are some of the elements of fruit-bearing that result from abiding in Christ according to these verses?

Verse 2—

Verse 4—

Verse 5—

Verse 8—

How are you challenged when you compare "more fruit" in verse 2 and "much fruit" in verse 8?

Spending Time in God's Word
What does Colossians 3:16 say about God's Word?

And Psalm 33:11?

Describe your time in God's Word this past week. For instance, what did you read? Was your time consistent? Was it daily?

Now create a plan and make a schedule for next week that includes spending time in God's Word. (Don't forget to be specific as you make your schedule.) What changes will you make?

Spending Time in Prayer

What does Mark 1:35 reveal about Jesus' habit of prayer?

And Luke 11:1?

Describe your time in prayer this past week. For instance, was your time consistent? Was it daily?

Now create a plan and make a schedule for next week that includes spending time in prayer. (Don't forget to be specific as you make your schedule.) What changes will you make?

Obeying God's Commands

What does John 15:10 say about Jesus' obedience to God's commands?

Can you point to any areas of obedience in your own walk with God where you need to follow in Jesus' steps?

Now, can you point to ways you plan to start down the path of obedience in these areas?

Renewing Our Commitment to Christ

Look up these scriptures in your Bible and note the truth of each:

Romans 3:23–

Romans 5:8–

Romans 6:23–

Romans 10:9–

Now, dear one, as we head into our study about a woman's walk with God and about growing in the fruit of the Spirit, are you alive? What is your answer? (Circle one.)

Yes   No   I'm not sure

Take time now for the most important step in your walk with God and settle with Him the certainty of your salvation—that you are indeed His child and alive in Christ!

Looking to God
for Love

Begin this lesson by reading the chapter in your book, *A Woman's Walk with God*, that's titled "Looking to God for Love." Note here any new truths or challenges that stand out to you.

Learning About Love

As we neared the end of Chapter One, I mentioned that the Holy Spirit *produces* His fruit of the Spirit in our lives as we *practice* obedience to His commands in the Bible. I also pointed out this teaching from Dr. John MacArthur:

> ~ Although we are commanded to exhibit
> spiritual fruit, it can never be produced except
> by yielding to the Holy Spirit. ~

I know we covered these commands regarding love in your book, but they're worth reviewing; so, look at these references in your Bible and write out the command given in each:

Ephesians 5:2–

John 15:12–

Titus 2:4–

Matthew 22:39–

Luke 6:27–

Now, where does God's kind of love come from according to these verses in your Bible?

1 John 4:7-8–

Romans 5:5–

Galatians 5:22–

With this foundational understanding of the commands *to* love and the source *of* love, let's look now at five principles from God's Word that can help us to walk in love.

Principle #1: *Love is an act of the will.*
How did God demonstrate His love in John 3:16?

And how did Jesus demonstrate His love in Matthew 20:28?

And in Luke 9:51?

Is there someone in your life you, by an act of your will, need to love today? And, specifically, how "will" you demonstrate that love?

~ Love is sharing a part
of yourself with others. ~

Principle #2: *Love is action—not just words.*
First John 3:18 has always spoken loudly to me about love. Look it up and share how it speaks to you.

How does the scenario in James 2:15-16 illustrate the principle of acts of love versus words of love?

So, are the people under your roof receiving your *words* of love ("Have a nice day! Remember Mom loves you!") or your *works* of love (three meals a day and clean clothes)? Explain your answer.

~ Works, not words, are the proof of love. ~

Principle #3: *Love reaches out to the unlovely.*

In a few words, how does God extend His love to all according to Matthew 5:43-45?

And in Luke 6:35a?

Is there any one person or group of persons that you fail to reach out to? Or is there anyone you are purposefully avoiding? What advice does Proverbs 3:27 have for you?

And what message and example does Romans 5:8 offer you?

Now, what will you do differently toward those you named above?

~ Kindness is the ability to love people
more than they deserve. ~

Principle #4: *We need God to help us love.*

I know we looked at Romans 5:5 once before, but look at it again and note the help God makes available to us.

Now you may want to pray along as you read this prayer and ask God to help you, too, to walk in the way of love.

> *A Prayer for Love*
> O my God, let me walk in the way of love
> which knoweth not how to seek self in
> anything whatsoever.
> But what love must it be? It must be
> an ardent love,
> a pure love,
> a courageous love,
> a love of charity,
> a humble love, and
> a constant love.
> O Lord, give this love into my soul, that I may
> never more live nor breathe but out of a more
> pure love of Thee, my All and only God.
> Amen.[3]

Principle #5: *Love expects nothing in return.*
Note how Luke 6:35 speaks to this principle.

Take this opportunity to look at 1 Corinthians 13:4-8, possibly the greatest definition of love ever written. Which quality of love fits Principle #5—love expects nothing in return, and why?

Galatians 6:10 also has a word for us. What is it?

Can you pinpoint any area where you are failing to show unselfish love? Or can you share an instance when you helped someone with no motive other than love?

A mother found under her plate one morning at breakfast a bill made out by her small son, Bradley, aged eight—

Mother owes Bradley:

For running errands	25 cents
For being good	10 cents
For taking music lessons	15 cents
For extras	5 cents
Total	55 cents

Mother smiled but made no comment. At lunch Bradley found the bill under his plate with 55 cents and another piece of paper neatly folded like the first. Opening it he read—

Bradley owes Mother:

For nursing him through scarlet fever	Nothing
For being good to him	Nothing
For clothes, shoes, and playthings	Nothing
For his playroom	Nothing
For his meals	Nothing
Total	Nothing[4]

Defining Love

Explain in your own words how *love is the sacrifice of self* defines biblical love. By all means, feel free to write your own definition or slogan for love based on what you've learned from the Bible.

Living Out Love

How does the illustration of watering flowers speak to you about living out or "pouring out" love...even to those who are *un*-lovely?

And, once again, *who* is the source of love?

I spoke of my watering ritual as "the bucket brigade." First I filled the bucket at the faucet, the source. How many ways can you think of for going to God, the Source of all things, so that He can fill your empty heart with His gracious love? I know I mentioned prayer. Can you think of other ways?

Love Lived Out by Ruth

Scan the story of Ruth and the marvelous love she demonstrated to her mother-in-law, the widow Naomi, in Ruth 2:1-23. Note some of the many loving "sacrifices of self" that Ruth made and then enjoy the definition of love according to the early church father Augustine.

> When asked what love looks like, Augustine replied,
> "Love has *hands* to help others.
> It has *feet* to hasten to the poor and needy.
> It has *eyes* to see misery and want.
> It has *ears* to hear the sighs and sorrow of men.
> This is what love looks like."

Love Lived Out in You

God gave Ruth to Naomi, a "Mara" (meaning bitter), a mother-in-law bereft of husband and sons. Yes, Naomi certainly needed love in her life! Now, who has God placed in *your* life that needs His love? And what will you do to be more sensitive (as Augustine's words above show us) and more giving?

Things to Do Today to Walk in Love

Note the four things I listed in this section of your book that you and I can begin doing today to walk in love. (And don't forget to look up the Bible references given.) As you make your list, note at least one thing you will do today in each area.

1. Remember the people at home (Titus 2:4)...

2. Remember to look to the Lord (1 John 4:7)...

3. Remember your assignment (Galatians 5:13)...

4. Remember Jesus (Matthew 20:28)...

5. May I add another "remember"? Remember the importance of the fruit of the Spirit love as noted by another...

The fruit of the Spirit begins with love. There are nine graces spoken of, and of these nine Paul puts love at the head of the list; love is the first thing, the first in that precious cluster of fruit. Someone has said that all the other eight can be put in terms of love.

> Joy is love exulting.
>
> Peace is love in repose.
>
> Patience is love on trial.
>
> Kindness is love in society.
>
> Goodness is love in action.
>
> Faith is love on the battlefield.
>
> Gentleness is love at school.
>
> Self-control is love in training.

So it is love all the way; love at the top, love at the bottom, and all the way along down this list of graces. If we only just brought forth the fruit of the Spirit, what a world we would have![5]

Offering the Sacrifice of Joy

Begin this lesson by reading the chapter in your book, *A Woman's Walk with God*, that is titled "Offering the Sacrifice of Joy." Note here any new truths or challenges that stand out to you.

What the Bible Says About Joy

In our culture we tend to think of joy as happiness, as a "feeling" that we enjoy when things are going our way, as a sense of elation and excitement. But you and I know that happiness and feelings and "the good life" are all temporary and conditional. Aren't you glad that as a woman who walks with God you can enjoy true spiritual joy regardless of life's conditions? Regardless of how you feel? Regardless of your situation?

Hear these fine words on the subject of joy versus happiness...

> Joy is distinctly a Christian word and a Christian thing. It is the reverse of happiness. Happiness is the result of what happens of an agreeable sort. Joy has its springs deep down inside. And that spring never runs dry, no matter what happens. Only Jesus gives that joy. He had joy, singing its music within, even under the shadow of the cross.[6]

Shortly before His trial, Jesus explained to His confused disciples what was about to happen. According to John 16:20 what
would be the response of His disciples to His crucifixion?

And what response would also accompany His resurrection?

To illustrate the sorrow/joy of verse 20, Jesus next pointed
to a naturally occurring event (verse 21). What was that
event? And can you share from your own experience how
such a painful occasion can produce such joy?

Let's look further and see what the Bible has to say about
God's fruit of the Spirit joy and several good reasons we can
be joyful…no matter what.

Reason #1—Our joy is permanent.
—What is the promise of John 16:22?

—And what is our role in experiencing God's joy?

Reason #2–Our joy is always available.

–According to Philippians 4:4, what is one way you can "tap into" God's ever-available joy?

Reason #3–Our joy is also inexpressible.

–How is our spiritual joy described in 1 Peter 1:8?

Summary–Write out the summarizing statement regarding spiritual joy given on page 45. Then write out how you plan, with the Lord's help, to remember this truth the next time you face a difficulty in life.

The Sources of Joy

As a Christian you have many sources of joy available to you. Let's consider these five guaranteed sources.

God Himself–is a powerful source of joy. How is God described in Psalm 43:4?

And what was Nehemiah's declaration in Nehemiah 8:10?

God's salvation–should give us joy, no matter where we are or what's happening to us. What does the prophet say that God has done for him in Isaiah 61:10, and what effect did it have on him?

God's promises–provide an unending source of joy. Jot down three of your favorite promises from the Bible and then note what King Solomon said about the promises of God in 1 Kings 8:56.

1.

2.

3.

Christ's kingdom–is yet another source of true spiritual joy. As people hear and respond to the gospel, what is their normal reaction (Acts 13:48-49)?

Our future in Christ–is most definitely another rich source of joy. What do these verses say awaits us in the future?

Psalm 16:11–

Revelation 21:4–

An Image of Joy

Whenever I teach through this section of *A Woman's Walk with God*, I always like to follow up the story of my daughter and the diamonds with a look at a particularly (and literally!) dark time in the life of Paul. Read about that dark time now in Acts 16:16-24. What facts make this a dark and dismal scenario? (List as many as you can.)

And how did Paul and his companion and fellow prisoner Silas handle their situation in verse 25? Or in what ways did they offer "the sacrifice of praise"?

And what effect did this "sacrifice" have on the other prisoners (verse 25)?

Now, can you share some current "dark" or difficult time in your life? Also share how offering the sacrifice of praise would bring "light" to your situation, enlightenment to others, and glory to God.

The Sacrifice of Praise

As we discussed previously, each fruit of the Spirit is commanded of you and me as God's children. Look now for yourself at these scriptures and jot down your observations about these commands that affect your joy:

Philippians 4:4–

1 Thessalonians 5:16 and 18–

How do these exhortations to rejoice and give thanks—no matter what—encourage you to offer the sacrifice of praise to God?

The Sounds of Joy

Oh, how Jim and I enjoyed our visit to that refreshing, gurgling brook on that cold day up in the High Sierras (pages 41-42)! That little brook issued forth the sounds of joy...regardless of the rocks that broke its surface, disturbed its tranquility, impeded its progress, and even altered its course forever.

And I do so appreciate the thought of Mrs. Spurgeon's old oak logs releasing their song and sacrifice as the fire raged round about them. They were literally singing in the fire!

How do these two illustrations further encourage you to lift the sweet sounds of joy even in your trials? (And after you've answered, don't forget to pour forth such sweet sounds out of *your* heart and lips!)

> The joy of life is living it and doing things of
>   worth,
> In making bright and fruitful all the barren
>   spots of earth.
> In facing odds and mastering them and rising
>   from defeat,
> And making true what once was false, and
>   what was bitter, sweet.
> For only he knows perfect joy whose little bit
>   of soil
> Is richer ground than what it was when he
>   began to toil.
>   —Edgar A. Guest

Hannah's Song of Joy

Hannah—the woman about whom nothing negative is reported in the Bible! Oh, to be a Hannah! Well, perhaps we, too, can learn to sing her song of joy. First, take a few minutes to read over Hannah's story in 1 Samuel 1:1–2:1. Then do the following exercise, laying your "problem" beside Hannah's and weighing your responses in the light of hers. Hopefully you can "check off" the godly responses!

Hannah's problem	Your problem
☑ quietly endured her pain	☐
☑ never acted out of vengeance	☐
☑ sought God through prayer	☐
☑ rejoiced as she offered her sacrifice	☐

The Supreme Model of Joy

"Jesus, Jesus, Jesus"…go the words to a familiar refrain we so love to sing! And Jesus demonstrates for us the supreme model of joy. Read from your own precious Bible Hebrews 12:2. How does "looking unto Jesus" and His example inspire you to joy?

Cultivating Joy

I mentioned a few of the commands for joy earlier (Philippians 4:4 and 1 Thessalonians 5:16 and 18). Now look at several others that bring us a powerful message about *how* to cultivate joy.

Psalm 34:1–

Hebrews 13:15–

James 1:2–

Which of these commands do you need to obey right now to cultivate joy in your situation?

Assignment for Joy

I asked as you were reading this chapter in your book that you name the trial that causes you the greatest grief, the sharpest pain, and the deepest sorrow. Now I want you to identify it and write it down.

Things to Do Today to Walk in Joy

Note the three things listed that you and I can begin doing today to walk in joy. (And don't forget to look up the Bible references given.) As you make your list, note at least one thing you will do today in each area.

1.

2.

3.

A Final Word About Joy
Take joy home,
And make a place in thy great heart for her,
And give her time to grow, and cherish her!
Then will she come and often sing to thee....[7]

4

Experiencing God's Peace

 Begin this lesson by reading the chapter in your book, *A Woman's Walk with God,* that is titled "Experiencing God's Peace." Note here any new truths or challenges that stand out to you.

As we step into this lesson about God's marvelous peace, consider this definition: "The peace of the New Testament… denotes the absence or end of all strife. It speaks of a state of untroubled, undisturbed well-being and the utmost of security. 'Peace' is not simply a matter of feeling safe and secure from one's enemies for the moment. It speaks of a feeling that one's enemies have been utterly destroyed and that safety and security are an everlasting possession."[8]

Understanding the Peace of the Lord

True spiritual peace comes with knowing that our heavenly Father is continually with us. Thoughtfully read Psalm 139:7-12. Then make a list of some of the many places and situations where God is continually with us.

Peace also comes when we acknowledge that God will supply our every need. What truths do these scriptures teach us?

2 Corinthians 12:9–

Philippians 4:19–

Trusting God

Everyone yearns for peace, but what is the truth taught in John 16:33?

The sacrifice of trust–that's how I attempt to define peace. What does Isaiah 26:3 have to say about peace and trusting God?

And Philippians 4:6-7?

Receiving God's Peace

Four sources of peace are available to you and me. Consider each of them as you jot down the truths about peace drawn from these verses.

God, the Son–according to Isaiah 9:6, what is one of the names of Jesus?

And what did Jesus, God's Son, accomplish (Romans 5:1)?

God, the Father–Isaiah 26:3

God's Word–Psalm 119:165

God, the Spirit–John 14:26

What are the situations in your life that tempt you most to fear, terror, panic, or dread?

Now that you're more familiar with the peace God and His Word extend to you, can you think of any reason not to trust in the Lord and enjoy God's peace *in* your situation? What will you do the next time you're prone to fear or worry?

Choosing the Peace of God over Panic

Take a moment to read over the accounts of Jesus and His disciples' adventure on the Sea of Galilee in Mark 4:35-41...

...and Luke 8:22-25.

What probing questions did Jesus ask of the Twelve in Mark 4:40?

Now, how does *your* fear reflect a lack of faith and trust in God? Jesus' disciples seemed to have forgotten that "their times were in God's hand." Look at Psalm 31:15 where this phrase originated. How does the fact of God's sovereign hand minister peace to your fretting soul? And in the situation you named above?

A personal note...this past year I've been studying through the Psalms, and in my personal journal I have three pages of notes from my readings on Psalm 31:15 regarding David's words, "My times are in Your hand." Let me share just a little of what I gleaned about verse 15 in my quiet times through this beloved Psalm 31.

—St. Augustine ordered a copy of Psalm 31 to be written out and placed where he could see and read it as he lay dying. He especially loved verses 5 and 15, reading, "Into Your hand I commit my spirit.... My times are in Your hand."9

—Dan Crawford was only 19 years old in 1889 when he ventured into central Africa for the first time. He served as a missionary for more than three decades and translated the Bible into Luba-Sanga. When Crawford died in 1926, the Old Testament had just been printed, and the national

Christians put a copy of the translation under his head when they buried him. Psalm 31:15 had been a particularly difficult challenge for Crawford to translate. Finally it was decided that the best way to put it into the language of the people would be like this:

> All my life's *whys* and *whens* and *wheres* and
> *wherefores* are in God's hands.[10]

Choosing the Peace of God When Pressure Mounts

"The whirlwind of life." I'm sure I don't have to explain that phrase to you! Read through the delightful and insightful tale of two sisters—Mary and Martha—in Luke 10:38-42. In your own words, how was Martha's *lack of peace* exhibited for all to see?

And by contrast, how did Mary's *peace* exhibit itself?

Now…for a look in the mirror that James 1:23 speaks of! How would you describe your walk with God in terms of offering the sacrifice of trust and enjoying God's peace? Or, put another way, are you a "Mary" or a "Martha"? Please explain your answers…and then enjoy the words below describing yet another "whirlwind" of life. And remember—this exercise is important!

In God's Hand
At the heart of the cyclone tearing the sky
And flinging the clouds and the towers by,
Is a place of central calm;
So here in the roar of mortal things,
I have a place where my spirit sings,
In the hollow of God's palm.[11]

"I'm Busy, Lord!"

Oh, what a debt we Christian women owe to poetess Nancy Stitzel! I know she expressed (page 71) so well *my* times of tension (and excuses). And based on my talks with many others just like you and me, Nancy has hit the nail on the head in terms of describing the problem...and in terms of the much-needed solution! Why not enjoy Nancy Stitzel's gift of words again and then "wait" upon the Lord...just like Mary did?

Walking on the Path of Peace

After looking at your answers to the questions regarding "choosing the peace of God when pressure mounts,"

–what will you do in the area of praying to God?

A Prayer for Peace
from *The Book of Common Prayer*

Most holy God, the source of all good desires, all right judgments, and all just works, give to us, Your servants, that peace which the world cannot give, so that our minds may be fixed on the doing of Your will, and that we, being delivered from the fear of all enemies, may live in peace and quietness; through the mercies of Christ Jesus our Savior. Amen.

—What will you do in the area of pausing before the Lord?

—What will you do in the area of perusing God's Word?

Things to Do Today to Walk in Peace

Have you yet identified your greatest challenge in this area of peace? If not, do so now.

How can you offer the sacrifice of trust right now?

In 1873 a man named Horatio Spafford encountered what was probably his greatest challenge in the area of peace—his four daughters were drowned at sea when the ship on which they were crossing the Atlantic Ocean was struck by another vessel and sank. Horatio Spafford stood hour after hour on the deck of the ship carrying him to rejoin his sorrowing wife in Cardiff, Wales. When the ship passed the approximate place where his precious daughters had drowned, Spafford received sustaining comfort from God that enabled him to offer up his sacrifice of trust as he wrote these now-famous words to the hymn that gives so many Christians today the peace of God that passes all understanding:

> *It Is Well with My Soul*
> When peace, like a river, attendeth my way,
> when sorrows like sea billows roll;
> whatever my lot, Thou hast taught me to say,
> It is well, it is well with my soul.
>
> My sin, oh, the bliss of this glorious thought!
> My sin, not in part but the whole,
> is nailed to the cross, and I bear it no more,
> praise the Lord, praise the Lord, O my soul!
>
> It is well with my soul,
> It is well, it is well with my soul.
> —Horatio G. Spafford[12]

Now write out your own prayer—or hymn—to God acknowledging that, truly, your times *are* in His all-capable, all-loving, all-powerful, all-wise, all-knowing hand!

My Personal Prayer for Peace

And now, dear one, as Aaron prayed when blessing the children of Israel,

A Benediction for Peace
The LORD bless you and keep you;
The LORD make His face to shine upon you,
and be gracious to you;
The LORD lift up His countenance upon you,
and give you peace.
—Numbers 6:24-26

5

Looking at Jesus' Attitudes

 Begin this lesson by reading the chapter in your book, *A Woman's Walk with God*, that is titled "Looking at Jesus' Attitudes." Note here any new truths or challenges that stand out to you.

I know we considered these scriptures that detail for us some of the events of Jesus' death, but there's no substitute for looking them up in your own Bible and reflecting on them…one by one.

The Plan

What announcement from Jesus set this part of God's plan for Jesus' death on the cross into motion—Matthew 26:17-18?

Following fellowship and prayer with His disciples, to where did Jesus retreat—John 18:1?

The Purpose

According to Jesus' own words in Matthew 20:28, what was the purpose of His life on earth?

And how do you rate in this area of your walk with God? For instance, reflect on the past 24 hours. Did you pour out your energy in sacrificial service to those who crossed your path? How did you fare at home…with your husband, children, in-laws, and neighbors? Or, if you have a job, was every encounter an opportunity to serve someone else?

Were there victories? Jot down one incident when God enabled you to exhibit Jesus' heart of service and sacrifice.

Were there any failures? Be specific as you sketch one here. What went wrong? And what could you do next time?

Take a minute to write out Matthew 20:28 on a card so that you can carry it with you and memorize it. Allow its truth to permeate your heart as you walk in the steps of Christ, your Savior!

The Place

Look again at the place of Matthew 26:36.

What does John 18:2 tell us about this particular place?

Other "places" of prayer are mentioned by Jesus or reflect His own prayer life. What do you learn about prayer from...

Matthew 6:6?

Mark 1:35?

Now describe your "place" of prayer.

How often do you visit your favorite place of prayer each week?

What will you do to be more regular in your visits there this next week?

And who can you be accountable to for your plan to do so?

Why not pay a visit to your place of prayer today?

The People

The lives of Jesus' twelve disciples make a wonderful study in themselves! In fact, a good exercise to do on your own is to read through the four Gospels and Acts 1 and make notes on the disciples' relationships, their personalities, their successes and failures, their strengths and weaknesses, and the lessons Jesus taught them. But for now, what do we learn about their time with Jesus in the Garden of Gethsemane—Matthew 26:36?

Unfortunately, "the people" who accompanied Jesus into this dark hour failed Him. What does Matthew 26:40 reveal about them?

And Matthew 26:43?

And Matthew 26:45?

Finally, what did the Twelve do as tensions mounted in Matthew 26:56?

And what did Peter do in Matthew 26:69-74?

And, saddest of all, how did the "worst" of the people nearest our Lord behave in Matthew 26:14-16 and Matthew 26:47-50?

The Problems

As we can see, Jesus was having problems with His disciples. And obviously, they were having their own problems, too! But there were other problems Jesus was dealing with in prayer. Note how the Bible describes Jesus' times of prayer:

Matthew 26:37-38–

Mark 14:33–

Luke 22:44–

Hebrews 5:7–

What command did Jesus give His disciples in Matthew 26:41?

And why?

Write out Jesus' prayer in Matthew 26:39.

What was the attitude of His heart?

The Process

It's clear that Jesus most definitely poured out the sacrifice of love for us! And to do so, He looked to the Father through prayer. And, as I pointed out in your book, this "was not the flinging of trite thoughts toward heaven" (page 79). What does Matthew 26:40 say was the duration of Jesus' *first* time at prayer?

What does Matthew 26:42-43 tell us about a *second* time of prayer?

And what does Matthew 26:44-46 tell us about a *third* time of prayer?

Beloved, all evidence leads us to conclude that Jesus' battle in prayer was likely three hour-long sessions of agonizing, wrestling, struggling, and fighting so that He could do all that God required of Him in fulfilling His purpose for His life…and death!

And *joy*? What does Hebrews 12:2 say about Jesus' joy in doing the Father's will?

And *peace*? What does Matthew 26:46 say Jesus confidently announced after his time(s) of prayer?

Prayer, dear one, is how we can walk with God through the circumstances and challenges of life…just like Jesus did.

> For love, we look to the Father.
> For joy, we lift the sacrifice of praise.
> For peace, we trust in the Lord.

The Product

After you've read over this section of your book, share in your own words how Jesus poured out His personal "sacrifice of self" on your behalf. Then thank Him profusely!

Now, dear one, what is God asking of you...in your rela-tionships...in your trials...in your life situation...in your afflictions? Note here one *problem* you are struggling with.

Are you willing to go through the *process* (agonizing prayer) to gain the *product* (a complete acceptance of God's will for your life)? Why or why not? And what's holding you back? For instance, do you merely need to spend time...or more time...in prayer? Or do you need to simply cease struggling and lift the sacrifice of praise to God and thank Him for His plan for your life? Or do you need to trust God more fully in order to bask in His peace that truly surpasses human understanding? Be specific. And then take action *now!*

The Performance

Evaluate your performance when it comes to following God's direction for your life.

Are you quick to go to prayer?

Are you quick to give praise and thanks?

Are you quick to trust the Lord?

What will you do to cultivate or advance these good habits of your walk with God?

For Love, for Love
Father of spirits, this my sovereign plea
I bring again and yet again to Thee.

Fulfill me now with love, that I may know
A daily inflow, daily overflow.

For love, for love, my Lord was crucified,
With cords of love He bound me to His side.

Pour through me now; I yield myself to Thee,
O Love that led my Lord to Calvary.
—Amy Carmichael[13]

6

Resisting in Patience

Begin this lesson by reading the chapter in your book, *A Woman's Walk with God*, that is titled "Resisting in Patience." Note here any new truths or challenges that stand out to you.

Beginnings

Begin this lesson by looking at and writing out these commands regarding patience:

–Ephesians 4:1-2

This book is about your walk with God. How would you characterize your walk with Him during the past 24 hours in this crucial and attention-needing area of resisting in patience? Be sure you explain your answer.

–Colossians 3:12

Check out your spiritual wardrobe, so to speak. Is the godly attitude of patience a prominent part of your adornment? Again, please explain. Then seek to "bundle up" in God's precious patience.

Bundle Up

Patience serves as a protection against wrongs as clothes do against cold. For if you put on more clothes, as the cold increases it will have no power to hurt you. So in like manner you must grow in patience when you meet with great wrongs, and they will then be powerless to vex your mind.

—Leonardo da Vinci

–Galatians 5:16 and 22

What solution and assistance does God offer us in the challenging area of patience?

Facing Up to the Challenge of People

As we step out on the path of growing in God's patience, can you pinpoint one (or two!) specific areas or relationships where you need God's gracious patience? For instance, is yours a busy, bustling household that seems to move only at high speed? Or is your walk each day accompanied by a handful of little people? Or do teenagers create a special need for God's patience? Or do you live with a husband who is stressed and irritable…which so often tempts you to stress and irritation yourself? Or do people and events at work challenge your patience? Describe your personal challenge now and write out your personal prayer of commitment, and then "commit" it (and *them*—the people, that is!) to God. Then let's see what we can learn about resisting in patience.

Personal challenge–

Prayer of commitment–

> We can rejoice, too, when we run into problems and trials for we know that they are good for us—they help us to learn to be patient. And patience develops strength of character in us and helps us trust God more each time we use it until finally our hope and faith are strong and steady (Romans 5:3-5 TLB).

The Meaning of Patience

As we try to grasp the meaning of godly patience, fill in each ingredient as described in your book. Then jot down the definitions and explanations that made patience more understandable to you.

Ingredient #1–

If you have a dictionary nearby, look up the word *endurance*. Write the meaning here, along with any statements from your book that helped your understanding.

~ Patience is accepting a difficult situation
without giving God a deadline to remove it. ~

Ingredient #2—

How is your patience quotient when pain is inflicted
upon you?

Ingredient #3—

Describe the mercy of God as revealed by His patience in
2 Peter 3:9.

Ingredient #4—

According to Romans 12:19, why are we not to worry
about or be involved in vengeance or retaliation against
those who hurt us?

Struggling for Patience

Now write out my slogan or motto on patience (page 92, top).

Also, if you would like to write your own slogan, do so. Just
be sure you keep it short so you can remember it...and use
it!

Looking at God's Instructions About Patience

Look now at a few examples of patience (some positive and some negative) from the Bible:

God was patient–After reading 1 Peter 3:20 and Genesis 6:3, write out a few words describing the patience of God.

Jesus was patient–What did Jesus say you and I are to do regarding our enemies in Luke 6:27-28?

How did Jesus exhibit patience toward those who put Him to death (Luke 23:34)?

According to 1 Peter 3:9, what else can we do that reflects a heart of patience?

Paul was patient–What does Paul say our behavior toward those who are not Christians is to be in 2 Timothy 2:24?

And why (2 Timothy 2:25-26)?

Who are the unbelievers whom God has placed in your life?
In your family? In your neighborhood? In your office? In
your dorm? In your class? Name them now...and then
transfer their names into your prayer journal or notebook as
a prompt for you to faithfully pray for them.

What will you do to look to God for His patience and
understanding and love for these people?

Sarah was not *patient*–Poor Sarah! Read about her impatience in Genesis 16:1-6. How did her treatment of Hagar
show a lack of patience?

Now look again at the four ingredients of patience. What
was lacking in Sarah's behavior?

Can you share a time when you acted like Sarah?

Hannah was patient–Oh, the lovely Hannah! Such a model
of so many virtues! Read about her difficult situation *and*
her difficult person in 1 Samuel 1:1-11,19-20. How did she
handle her problems? And what evidences of the ingredients of patience do you witness in her walk with God?

Waiting for the Judge

Read about the unfortunate situation some early Christians faced in James 5:1-6. What a scathing warning to wealthy unbelievers who mistreat those that belong to Christ! What do you learn about the believers in verse 6?

Now read James 5:7-11. Make a brief list of James's instructions to these Christians on how to suffer and wait with patience.

In your own words, what are some things James says about patience?

And what is (or will be) the role of the judge?

What, dear one, can you do today, in your particular framework or circumstances, to wait?

Things to Do Today to Walk in Patience

We can thank God that He always gives us practical advice and "how-to's" in His Word. Here are just a few useful helps for cultivating God's fruit of the Spirit patience in your everyday walk.

–Train yourself in long-suffering. How does Proverbs 19:11 challenge you?

–Lengthen your fuse. Read 1 Corinthians 13:4 and then make plans to lengthen your fuse!

–Remove opportunities to sin. How can you follow God's advice found in Romans 13:14?

–Follow Jesus' example. According to 1 Peter 2:22-23, what was Jesus' response to suffering? And what can you do to follow in His steps (verse 21)?

–Pray. As Jesus showed us in 1 Peter 2:23, prayer is one sure way to resist in patience. Why not pray now? Commend yourself and your problem situation and/or people to Him. Purpose, too, to turn to God in prayer—as many times as it takes—each time you need His patience today!

~ Patience is the best remedy
for most trouble. ~

Now, my dear friend, go make a pearl—a priceless pearl of patience! And rejoice!

> The most extraordinary thing about the oyster is this: Irritations get into his shell. He does not like them. But when he cannot get rid of them, he uses the irritation to do the loveliest thing an oyster ever has a chance to do—he makes a pearl.
>
> If there are irritations in our lives today, there is only one prescription: make a pearl. It may have to be a pearl of patience, but, anyhow, make a pearl.
>
> —Harry Emerson Fosdick

7

Planning for Kindness

 Begin this lesson by reading the chapter in your book, *A Woman's Walk with God*, that is titled "Planning for Kindness." Note here any new truths or challenges that stand out to you.

Our Calling to Kindness

As we've found commands on each fruit of the Spirit, so now we find commands in the Bible for kindness. What do these scriptures tell us about acting in kindness? Also note *who* is to receive our kindness.

–Ephesians 4:32

–Colossians 3:12

–2 Timothy 2:24

What steps are you taking each day to "put on a heart of kindness"?

Defining Kindness

Now write out my definition or slogan for kindness.

And, if you'd like, write out your own slogan. Remember to keep it short, simple, and to the point!

Learning from Opposites

Looking at opposites—what something is *not*—is a good tool for learning what something *is*. Read these scriptures and note what you can learn about kindness from the opposite trait being portrayed.

Arguing—
Galatians 5:19-20–

2 Timothy 2:24–

James 3:14-15–

Chafing—

Read Matthew 11:28-30 for yourself. What picture is Matthew painting here, and what message do you receive regarding kindness?

Cultivating Kindness

As I mentioned in the book, a simple prayer prompt led me to conviction regarding kindness and to the pursuit of kindness in my heart and in my walk with God. The prompt simply suggested that I "pray for greater love and compassion for others." We can thank God that His Word tells us exactly how to pursue and cultivate kindness!

Caring is a part of kindness—

Each Sunday when I plan for the upcoming week, I include plans to care. Does that sound strange? Well, let me explain. I jot down the names of those that I want to remember to extend kindness to during the week—best friends, family members, special people (perhaps those grieving a loss), and *those* special people (the ones Jesus labels as enemies!). Then I plan at least one act of kindness I'll do for each person during the week. This is truly planning to be kind! And it does help to cultivate a caring heart in me and hopefully blesses others.

Now for you. Look over the suggestions made in your book regarding caring. How will you plan to show some kindness this week? And who will your special target people be? Plan now for kindness and for caring.

Thinking is a part of kindness—

Look at the touching story of David's plans for kindness in 2 Samuel 9:1-7. Beloved, this took some thinking! Now, who are the ones you think about or should think about?

And what does Philippians 2:3-4 have to say about our thoughts toward others?

Noticing is a part of kindness—

According to Proverbs 20:12, what "gifts" has God given to you?

Rebekah—Read Genesis 24:15-20 and describe what Rebekah noticed. (And please note—verse 10 tells us that this man had ten [!!!] camels).

The Shunammite woman—Read 2 Kings 4:8-10 and describe what the Shunammite woman noticed.

Dorcas—Read Acts 9:36-39 and describe what Dorcas had noticed.

Jesus–Read Mark 6:32-36 and describe what Jesus noticed. (And please "notice" the behavior of Jesus' disciples as they failed to exhibit the fruit of kindness!)

Little Things
Look around you, first in your own family,
then among your friends and neighbors, and
see whether there be not someone whose
little burden you can lighten, whose
little cares you may lessen, whose
little pleasures you can promote, whose
little wants and wishes you can gratify.
—Unknown, 1852

Touching is a part of kindness–

Read these scriptures for yourself. How did Jesus teach us about touching in these instances? (Also, where others were involved, note their behavior, too.)

–Matthew 20:29-34

–Mark 10:13-16

–Luke 5:12-13

–Luke 7:12-15

–Luke 13:10-17

Becoming Too Nice

Did you enjoy the story of my friend Judy who was considered to be "too nice"? Now, how can you look to the Lord and set about to plan for kindness so that you, too, just may well be thought of as being "too nice"?

Things to Do Today to Walk in Kindness

Kindness begins in your heart, dear one. And it is as you and I look to God for *His* kindness, for *His* grace, for *His* fruit in our life, that we begin to manifest the life of Christ *in* us. So here are a few suggestions—both spiritual and practical—to help you begin to cultivate and nurture the kindness of the Lord in your life.

–Pray for your enemies.

Read again Jesus' instructions in Luke 6:27-36 and list the responses we are to have toward our enemies. Also explain *why* Jesus said we are to do these things. Then bow your head and begin the process by praying for your enemies.

–Spend time with God.

And while you're in prayer, confess any ill will, bitterness, resentment, or grudges held against any individuals or groups who have wronged you in the past. Clear the slate, so to speak, with God. As David asked of God in prayer, "Create in me a clean heart, O God" (Psalm 51:10). Then purpose to plan for kindness toward those who have hurt you.

–Ask God for help.

Would you describe yourself as a kind person? Is yours a heart of compassion? Are you marked out and known for your concern for others? Explain why or why not. Put your finger on what is missing. For instance, are you just too busy to think about others? (That's why I plan for kindness on my weekly schedule! I found that in the busyness of life I wasn't thinking of others as much as I should.) Or is your heart stone cold? Or is your attention focused on yourself instead of on others? As I said, explain why or why not. Then ask God for His help.

–Study Jesus' life.

Oh, the beauty of the perfect and perfectly kind life of our dear Lord! Did you know that if you read just one chapter of the Gospels (Matthew, Mark, Luke, and John) each day you will read through the life of Christ four times a year? Why not purpose (and plan) to read a chapter a day (for even three months–that's one time through His life). And keep a little notebook or running list or make a journal entry each day of the times and ways Jesus demonstrated kindness. His, my friend, was a perfect heart of compassion and care!

For now, review the instances from this chapter in your book where His actions defined kindness.

—Make an effort at home.

A quote and a concept that has always challenged me on the home front is this: "God has no greater ground for those who are not faithful where they are." So where is kindness to be practiced first? Right at home. Each of us lives somewhere. And most of us live with someone else. We have parents and siblings, husbands and children, elderly grandparents, maybe even roommates. So this is obviously the "ground" where our grooming in kindness begins. Does your "plan" for the day and the week begin with kindnesses to be lived out at home? Answer—and plan for it—here! And don't worry about whether or not those nearest you *deserve* your kindness, for as the quote from the book defined kindness,

> ~ Kindness is the ability to love people
> more than they deserve. ~

—Pray for compassion.

As you can tell by now, this entire book about your walk with God is about looking to God for His fruit in your life. So, once again, pray for compassion! And, once again, as my prayer prompt advised, "pray for greater love and compassion for others." That's what St. Francis of Assisi did in these lines from his famous prayer:

Lord, grant that I may seek rather
To comfort—than to be comforted;
To understand—than to be understood;
To love—than to be loved.

8

Giving in Goodness

 Begin this lesson by reading the chapter in your book, *A Woman's Walk with God*, that is titled "Giving in Goodness." Note here any new truths or challenges that stand out to you.

Reviewing Our Progress

Take a few minutes to jot down the slogans or mottos or definitions that we've considered for these two fruit of the Spirit. If you wrote your own definitions, write them down, too. Also, in a sentence or two, write out your understanding of each.

Patience—

Kindness—

Getting a Handle on Goodness

As stated in your book, bearing the fruit of goodness will be easier if we understand three aspects of the biblical definition of spiritual goodness, aspects that relate to our conduct toward others.

First, true goodness is spiritual in its origin.

Look now at these scriptures and write out what they teach us about the goodness of God:

    –Psalm 33:5

    –Psalm 100:5

    –Nehemiah 9:25 and 35

When Moses asked to see God, how did God answer in Exodus 33:19?

On the contrary, what does the Bible teach us about the goodness of man (Romans 3:10 and 12)?

And what did the apostle Paul have to say on this subject (Romans 7:18-19)?

Second, goodness is active.

For the best illustration of this truth, we must look to Jesus! What does Acts 10:38 say about Him?

> Goodness is
> love in action,
> love with its hand to the plow,
> love with the burden on its back,
> love following His footsteps
> who went about continually doing good.
> —James Hamilton

Third, goodness is a readiness to do good.

Write out the slogan or definition given in your book regarding goodness.

And, as in the case of the previous fruit of the Spirit, feel free to write out your own short saying.

Did you enjoy John Wesley's rule of goodness to live by? Well, here's another theologian's perspective on goodness.

> The supreme test of goodness is not in the greater but in the smaller incidents of our character and practice; not what we are when standing in the searchlight of public scrutiny, but when we reach the firelight flicker of our homes; not what we are when some clarion-call rings through the air, summoning us to fight for life and liberty, but our attitude when we are called to sentry-duty in the grey morning, when the watch-fire is burning low.[14]
>
> —F. B. Meyer

Getting a Handle on Walking in Goodness

This seems like a good place to consider some of the Bible's commands for us to *walk*. Look up these scriptures and note the commands:

Romans 6:4—*walk...*

Galatians 5:16—*walk...*

Ephesians 4:1—*walk...*

Ephesians 5:2—*walk...*

Ephesians 5:8—*walk...*

Colossians 2:6–*walk*...

1 Thessalonians 2:12–*walk*...

1 John 2:6–*walk*...

We've been learning that each fruit of the Spirit is commanded of us as well as produced by the Holy Spirit in our lives. After this exercise of noticing these commands to *walk*, what choices do you need to begin making so that your *walk* is "in a manner worthy of the God who calls you"?

Choosing Goodness

I hope you enjoyed the real-life examples of my friends and students about their decisions to choose goodness. Now, for you...

...Is there any one behavior you can point to that does not honor the Lord? Your book mentioned blowing up, letting someone "have it" verbally, seething in anger, and a few other choice sins! How are these faults opposed to the patience, kindness, and goodness that God calls us to walk in and that honor and glorify Him? This is an important exercise, so please take the time to take it seriously.

Recognizing Goodness as an Assignment from God

We looked at some of God's commands to *walk*. Now let's look at some of His commands for *goodness*. Indeed, you'll find that goodness is an assignment from God!

Ephesians 2:8-10—How is our assignment from God spelled out here? (And don't miss the means of fulfilling and working out His assignment!)

Galatians 6:10—What is our calling here? And what groups of people are included in the command?

Luke 6:27-28—Now here's a tall order for goodness! Who is to receive God's goodness through us, according to these verses? Also, what is one key Jesus gives us here for following through on His command for goodness?

Putting Goodness to Work

All Christians are called to goodness. But God in His Word points out goodness and good works as having a special place in our lives as Christian *women*. Pay special attention to these scriptures that speak to us as women and note the value God places on His goodness in us.

Titus 2:3–

Titus 2:5–

1 Timothy 2:9-10–

1 Timothy 5:9-10–

Before we move on, do you see any areas in your life where you need to pay closer attention to goodness and good works? Put another way, do others think of *you* as a woman dedicated to every good work? Are "good works" what you're known for? Please explain. And while you're at it, make notes for changes and improvements! For, indeed, goodness is one of God's high callings to us as women.

Enjoying a Sampling of Goodness

Many of the women in the Bible show us God's goodness in their actions...as they truly *did everything* they could to ease the lives of others. How do you witness goodness lived out in these women?

Dorcas–We noticed Dorcas's kindness regarding the widows' needs. What did her goodness do about them in Acts 9:36-39?

The Shunammite woman–We also noticed the Shunammite's kind concern for God's prophet Elisha. What did her goodness do about his needs in 2 Kings 4:8-10?

Rebekah–And we noticed Rebekah's kind consideration of Abraham's servant. How did Rebekah's goodness go to work, so to speak, on behalf of the servant's needs, according to Genesis 24:15-20?

Lydia–Note the active goodness in this wonderful woman in Acts 16:11-15. What did she offer to Paul and Silas? And also in Acts 16:40?

Martha–I'm sorry, but I can't resist this one negative example, because I think in Martha we witness the right thing...done in the wrong way! Look at Luke 10:38-42 and see how Martha failed in her good deeds.

Learning from Jesus' Goodness

As always, Jesus is our most wonderful example of goodness. As God in the flesh, He truly went about doing good (Acts 10:38). For an example of His goodness to His enemies, read this scenario:

Luke 9:51-56–How did the disciples fail in goodness...and how did Jesus show them a better way? Then ask yourself, dear one: Is there any person in your life you would like to "call down fire" upon? What can you do to take upon yourself Jesus' gracious attitude and actions and give in goodness instead?

Walking in Goodness

Read again and pay careful attention to the statement by Oswald Chambers in this section of our chapter on giving in goodness. Then take these steps with a pure heart:

Confess what is unkind. A failure to be kind and give in goodness is a failure to walk by the Spirit. You and I must take such failures seriously. God does!

Take the initiative. Who do you know that needs your gift of goodness today? Your gift of God's love? Take the initiative and make the giving of the gift of goodness a priority.

Forget your own comfort. Just like Jesus, we are here to serve (Matthew 20:28)…whether it "feels" comfortable or not. Pray to regard others more highly than yourself and to set yourself aside and look instead on the needs of others.

Advance the happiness of others. What a blessing we as God's women can be to others when we have their welfare in mind and promote their well-being!

Things to Do Today to Walk in Goodness

Who needs your goodness today? Many souls cross your path each day who can benefit greatly from your gift of goodness. Plus *you* can benefit and grow in your walk with God as you look to Him for such grace, especially toward those who cause you pain. Oh, dear one, don't *you* as a woman who walks with God shut down your heart! Don't *you* succumb to returning evil for evil (1 Peter 3:9)! Paul pleads with you and me, "Do not be overcome with evil, but *you* overcome evil with good" (Romans 12:21, emphasis added).

You must "do good to those who hate you"
(Luke 6:27).

9

Looking at
Jesus' Actions

Woman's Walk WITH GOD

Begin this lesson by reading the chapter in your book, *A Woman's Walk with God*, that is titled "Looking at Jesus' Actions." Note here any new truths or challenges that stand out to you.

Acts 10:38 says of Jesus, He "went about doing good." As we wrap up our study of "The Actions of Patience, Kindness, and Goodness" and turn our attention to the perfect actions that were perfectly lived out by our perfect Jesus, take to heart the following insight into Jesus' goodness and seek to follow in His footsteps:

> Our Lord's mode of doing good sets forth His incessant activity! He did not only the good which came close to hand, but He "went about" on His errands of mercy. Throughout the whole land of Judea there was scarcely a village or a hamlet which was not gladdened by the sight of Him. How this reproves the creeping, loitering manner in which many professors serve the Lord. Let us gird up the loins of our mind, and be not weary in well doing.
> —Charles Spurgeon

The Scene

As we begin to look at Jesus' actions reflecting patience, kindness, and goodness, please refresh your memory of the events in the Garden of Gethsemane. Consider again these details describing Jesus' night of prayer.

How many times does Matthew record that Jesus prayed, and for possibly what duration (Matthew 26:39-44)?

What was Jesus' request of His disciples (Matthew 26:38 and 41), and what did they do instead while Jesus agonized in prayer (Matthew 26:40 and 43 and 45)?

When Jesus finished praying and emerged from His place of prayer, what did He announce to the disciples (Matthew 26:46)?

As we learned in our section on Jesus' attitudes:

For *love* He looked to the Father as He went forth to pour out His life a sacrifice for others, including us.

For *joy* He looked to the Father and, for the *joy* that was set before Him (Hebrews 12:2), went forth to fulfill His Father's will.

For *peace* He looked to the Father, trusted in Him, announced, "Let us be going," and went forth to die.

The Traitor

But…people were waiting for Jesus on the other side of the low rock wall around the Garden of Gethsemane. And one of those people was Judas, *the traitor*. What did Jesus say about him in Matthew 26:46?

And in John 13:18?

Look at Psalm 41:9 and then at Matthew 26:50. What greeting was given to Judas?

The word spoken by Jesus in Matthew 26:50 means "comrade or companion." How does this greeting by Jesus fulfill the definition of goodness?

The Mob

Read the account of the confrontation with the mob in John 18:4-9. How did Jesus live out...

...patience?

...kindness?

...goodness?

The Fleshly Response

We have already been exposed to Peter's actions in the garden, where he failed to exhibit the fruit of the Spirit. Now let's follow him into the courtyard of Caiaphas, the high priest, and see how his "deeds of the flesh" continue. Read Matthew 26:69-75 and write out a brief summary of Peter's fleshly behavior.

It seems that when we start moving down a certain path of "fleshly"conduct, things go from bad to worse. This was truly seen in Peter's actions the night of his denial of Jesus. What lessons can you take to heart from Peter's conduct on that most horrid of nights?

The Godly Response

In the book, we examined the betrayal account in Matthew 26. Having now looked at John 18, put the two accounts together and summarize how Jesus responded both to Judas and to the mob.

The godly response of patience–

The godly response of kindness–

The godly response of goodness–

Our Response

This chapter is titled "Looking at Jesus' Actions." Jesus truly is our model of godly behavior. He is also our source of strength for that behavior (see Philippians 4:13). So, when life would seem to pressure us to conform to a fleshly pattern of behavior, let's look to our Savior, Jesus. Before we are tempted to respond in an ungodly manner—in impatience, in ill will, or in the harmful treatment of another—let's wait on Jesus.

> Waiting on Jesus when I am weak,
> Claiming His promise to those who seek;
> Waiting on Jesus when I am strong,
> Trusting Him only all the day long.
>
> Waiting on Jesus when I'm opprest,
> Finding in Him sweet comfort and rest;
> Trusting Him fully, whate'er befall,
> Jesus my Saviour, Jesus my all.
>
> Waiting on Jesus lest I despair,
> Knowing He ever heareth my prayer;
> How can I doubt Him when He is near?
> No one so loving, no one so dear.
>
> Refrain:
> Waiting on Jesus, rapture divine!
> Wonder of wonders, Jesus is mine;
> Trusting and praying, whate'er betide,
> Walking each moment close by His side.[15]
> —Oswald J. Smith

10

Following Through
in Faithfulness

 Begin this lesson by reading the chapter in your
book, *A Woman's Walk with God*, that is titled
"Following Through in Faithfulness." Note here any
new truths or challenges that stand out to you.

How does the phrase "We have met the enemy—and they is
us" apply to a situation in your life? Or, put another way,
how are you sometimes your own worst enemy?

As we step into this third and final section of our study
about your walk with God, take a few moments to note the
path we've already considered. How has what you've been
reading and studying about God's spiritual fruit of Galatians
5:22-23 instructed you about better *attitudes* in the areas of
love, joy, and peace?

And how have your *actions*—reflecting patience, kindness,
and goodness—toward others begun to change?

Insights into Faithfulness

Here's a thoughtful insight into the definition of *faithfulness*:

> The seventh fruit of the Spirit is the word for standing fast, for steadfastness. It is the quality of reliability, trustworthiness, which makes a person one on whom we can utterly rely and whose word will stand....Faithfulness speaks of endurance, also—a firmness of purpose, especially amid danger and calamities.[16]

What part of this definition stands out the most to you or gives you reason to re-evaluate your own walk by the Spirit? Please explain.

Read Matthew 25:14-30. Where is Jesus while speaking this parable?

How does the prudence of the five virgins in the preceding parable (verses 1-13) relate to this one?

Insight #1—The God of Faithfulness

One of my favorite hymns, which speaks to the faithfulness of God, may be familiar to you as well. The author of this hymn of exaltation, Thomas Chisholm, wrote these words shortly before his death: "My income has never been large at any time due to impaired health in the earlier years which has followed me on until now. But I must not fail to record here the unfailing faithfulness of a covenant-keeping God and that He has given me many wonderful displays of His providing care which have filled me with astonishing grate-fulness." As you hum your way through this majestic hymn about our majestic God and His majestic faithfulness, you may want to express your own gratefulness.

> Great is Thy faithfulness, O God my Father;
> there is no shadow of turning with Thee;
> Thou changest not, Thy compassions,
>   they fail not;
> as Thou hast been, Thou forever wilt be.

> Great is Thy faithfulness!
> Great is Thy faithfulness!
> Morning by morning new mercies I see;
> all I have needed Thy hand hath provided;
> great is Thy faithfulness, Lord, unto me![17]

You and I can be thankful for people such as Thomas Chisholm, who thought at length about God's faithfulness and was able to move us to do the same! How should our knowledge of the faithfulness of God affect our faithfulness?

Insight #2—The Core of Faithfulness
Faithfulness has two aspects. Faithfulness to God and faith-fulness to _____.

Can you evaluate your faithfulness in the second category?

Insight #3—The Marks of Faithfulness

As you inventoried your own walk, which of the marks of faithfulness need further attention, and why?

Insight #4—The Opposites of Faithfulness

Relate a time when someone else was "unreliable" when you were counting on them. How can the memories and ramifications of that event encourage you to be more faithful when others are relying on you?

Insight #5—The Essence of Faithfulness

Write out here the slogan for faithfulness given in your book.

How can the resolve of this slogan help you to be more faithful?

Can you think of a few areas where you can look to the Lord for His help in putting our slogan to work in your life and in your relationships today?

The Need for Faithfulness

List one action you can take to be more faithful in the areas where God has placed you.

–As a Christian

–As a wife

–As a mother

–As a daughter

–As a home manager

–As a worker

–As a servant in the church

–As a friend

–As a neighbor

God has situated each one of us in our "place" in life. Now we must ask, "How am I minding my place?" Ask and answer this helpful question, jot down notes to yourself, spend time in prayer about your answers, and then enjoy the wise exhortation of another regarding your "place."

Mind Your Place
Is your place a small place?
Tend it with care!—He set you there.
Is your place a large place?
Guard it with care—He set you there.
Whate'er your place, it is
Not yours alone, but His
Who set you there.[18]
—John Oxenham

The Struggle to Be Faithful

We all struggle in our flesh to be faithful to the many roles and responsibilities that God has called us to. Which one(s) of the areas below do you struggle with the most? Describe the struggle in more detail and then write out how the "three-step operation" of *desire, looking to God,* and *following God's Word* can help you enjoy greater spiritual victory.

Tiredness—

Laziness—

Hopelessness—

Procrastination—

Rationalization—

Apathy—

Rebellion—

Women Who Were Faithful to Jesus

As you read about this faithful band of women, what acts of their faithfulness encouraged you most or set a good model for you to follow?

How does the faithfulness of the women who followed Jesus spur you on to be even more faithful?

Walking in Faithfulness

Re-read the following verses in your Bible. Which ones give you the most encouragement to be faithful? Why not commit several to memory?

Psalm 138:3

Proverbs 31:27

Luke 16:10

1 Corinthians 9:27

Philippians 4:13

1 Timothy 3:11

The Hero

I trust and pray that "The Hero" encouraged your faithfulness. Not many of us desire to be a "hero" but all of us
should desire to be faithful. Faithfulness starts with the little
things and the little areas of our lives. It's as simple as
keeping a promise or being on time for an appointment. It's
as simple as paying the bills promptly or following through
on an assignment. Faithfulness is as simple as "being where

you're supposed to be…doing what you're supposed to do."
The greatest words that we should long to hear from our
blessed Lord when we see Him face to face are these:

Well done, good and faithful servant;
you have been faithful over a few things,
I will make you ruler over many things.
Enter into the joy of your lord
(Matthew 25:23).

11

Growing Strong Through Gentleness

Begin this lesson by reading the chapter in your book, *A Woman's Walk with God*, that is titled "Growing Strong Through Gentleness." Note here any new truths or challenges that stand out to you.

The Meaning of Gentleness

Every woman who walks with God desires to imitate the gentleness of our Lord Jesus Christ. Consider now the facets that make up the meaning of the fruit of the Spirit gentleness.

1. *Gentleness means trusting the Lord*–In the book I asked a series of questions regarding showing forth the fruit of gentleness in your life. Now that you've thought about this precious quality of gentleness, answer these questions.

–In what areas of your life do you fail to show the fruit of gentleness?

–Where are you failing to submit to God and His management of your life?

–Do you consider *meekness* to be weakness?

–Do you generally bear grudges against others, contemplate revenge, think vengeful thoughts?

–Or are you learning to look beyond the injury inflicted by another, looking instead to God?

Whisper a prayer to God and ask His blessings as you seek to bear any harshness in life, trusting in Him.

Read Psalm 60:12. Can you describe an instance where you allowed God to fight your battle? What happened?

2. *Gentleness means submitting to the Master*–The gentle person is under the control of another. She is not fighting or struggling *with* her life or the issues that arise *in* her life. She obediently conforms to the wishes of others, because ultimately she is submissive to the wishes of her Master, the Lord Jesus Christ.

–What are some areas where your life could be characterized as wild and out of control?

–How can you begin to "submit to the wishes of your Master" to be "tamed"?

3. *Gentleness means following Christ's example*–How does the picture of Jesus, "King of kings and Lord of lords" (Revelation 19:16) riding into Jerusalem on a colt, the foal of a donkey, further illustrate for you the meaning of gentleness?

4. *Gentleness means bowing the soul*–I used the analogy of the shock of grain to illustrate how maturity is determined. What stage of spiritual development would you consider yourself to be in with respect to gentleness—newly planted, young sprout, maturing shock, fully mature? Please explain your answer.

5. *Gentleness means putting on a gentle spirit*–As I said in the book, gentleness requires a decision from us. In 1 Peter 3:1-6, the apostle Peter describes what a gentle woman, a woman with a meek and quiet spirit, looks like. What decisions have you made with respect to the following elements?

The element of submission–

The element of behavior–

The element of the heart–

The element of trust–

The element of faith–

6. *Gentleness means "take it"*–What was your initial response to this slogan for gentleness? Has your thinking changed toward this slogan? Why or why not?

Consider these examples from the Bible of some who learned what it meant to "take it," to look to God for His gentleness in their trying situations.

The apostles–Acts 5:40-41

Stephen–Acts 7:54-60

Paul and Silas–Acts 16:22-25

Servants to both good and harsh masters–1 Peter 2:18-21

The Posture of Gentleness

How does the picture of trust from Proverbs 3:5 and the admonition from Psalm 46:10 further clarify your understanding of gentleness?

Now, how do these two "postures" challenge you to assume a better posture of gentleness?

Demonstrations of Gentleness

In your own words describe how these men and women demonstrated gentleness.

Hannah–

Mary, the mother of Jesus–

Mary of Bethany–

Moses–

Yes, But How?

I'm sure by now you have taken the "giant first step" of identifying the greatest issue in your life. Now, have you applied these principles to your problem as you walk in gentleness?

1. Accept–

2. Pray–

3. Refuse to complain or grumble–

4. Refuse to manipulate–

Taking the First Step

If you have not yet identified the "great" issue in your life, or you have yet to apply the above four principles, write out how you will begin today to take a first step—even a tiny one.

Dear one, don't miss out on tapping into God's gentleness, the strongest force in the world!

Gentleness is the strongest force in the world, and
the soldiers of Christ are to be priests and to fight
the battle of the kingdom, robed, not in jingling
shining armor or with sharp swords,
nor with fierce and eager bitterness of controversy,
but in the meekness which overcomes.[19]
—Alexander Maclaren

12

Winning the Battle of Self-Control

 Begin this lesson by reading the chapter in your book, *A Woman's Walk with God*, that is titled "Winning the Battle of Self-Control." Note here any new truths or challenges that stand out to you.

God always acts and behaves in a way that is consistent with His nature. He perfectly controls His actions. This perfect control was modeled for us by Jesus Christ, God in human flesh, who lived a life of complete self-control. Hear what another has said of His example:

> In His incarnation Christ was the epitome of self-control. He was never tempted or tricked into doing or saying anything that was not consistent with His Father's will and His own divine nature.[20]

Look now at Matthew 4:1-11, which relates an incident in the life of Jesus where He exhibited self-control. In what areas of Jesus' life did the devil tempt Him? (See also 1 John 2:15-17 for help in answering this question.)

Matthew 4:1-4–

Matthew 4:5-7—

Matthew 4:8-11—

What defense did Jesus use to combat the temptations of the devil?

After looking at this one example from the life of Christ, what lessons can you learn about resisting your own temptations?

The devil has been a liar from the beginning and "the father of lies" (John 8:44). How did the devil (the serpent) tempt Eve in Genesis 3:1-5? (And do you notice any similarities to the tactics he used against Jesus?)

How does the statement "Perfect holiness possesses perfect control" give you further insight into your own spiritual walk and your struggles with self-control?

Reviewing God's Fruit

In your own words describe how self-control can assist you with respect to the other eight fruit of the Spirit.

Love–

Joy–

Peace–

Patience–

Kindness–

Goodness–

Faithfulness—

Gentleness—

What Is Self-Control?

Self-control is such an important concept to understand and to implement. Here is an additional quote that should help motivate us to seek God's help in controlling all areas of our life.

> The command of one's self is
> the greatest empire a man [or woman] can aspire unto,
> and consequently, to be subject to our own passions is
> the most grievous slavery.
> —John Milton

When Is Self-Control Needed?

Earlier you described how self-control was needed in your spiritual walk. Now describe how self-control is needed to combat the deeds of the flesh (Galatians 5:17).

What Does Self-Control Do?

In your book I suggested that you follow my friend's example and write out the list of strengths found on page 190 and use them as a checklist in areas where self-control is needed. If you are still struggling with some of these areas in your life and have not made the checklist, write them out now. Then find someone to hold you accountable.

Also please enjoy the thoughts of this writer on both faith-fulness *and* self-control:

Acts of faithfulness are the golden threads which make the lustre of a fruitful life. There is unity in such a life. It is a life consecrated through and through. Every act of faithfulness is the outburst and expression of the Life of the Spirit. They are like precious stones which the soul builds into its habitation for eternity. Our life is not made up of sudden bursts of inspiration, but of progressive efforts of daily fidelity. Even as the pasture land is made up of blades of grass, so the qualities of a faithful life, the solid strength of character, is not the outcome of one act but the result of a life of self-restraint.

—Ivor Rosser

What Does Self-Control Not Do?

To help us better understand God's desires for you and me not to give in to the flesh, I added scriptures to the list of "nots." Be sure you look up each one of them in your Bible and note God's message to you from each.

• Self-control does not yield to temptation (Romans 6:12).

• Self-control does not give in to desires (Galatians 5:16).

• Self-control does not participate in sin (Romans 6:13).

• Self-control does not indulge itself (1 Corinthians 10:31).

• Self-control does not satisfy itself (Galatians 5:24).

What Is a Slogan for Self-Control?

Relate a recent battle with self-control where the slogan "don't do it" helped. Or, put another way, how has the slogan "don't do it" helped you gain the victory in a recent battle of self-control?

Learning from Others About Self-Control

David shows us self-control in the two instances when he spared Saul's life (1 Samuel 24:3-7; 26:7-9). What reason was behind David's self-control (1 Samuel 24:8-15; 26:10)?

How could this same dependence upon God help you the next time you need self-control?

Unfortunately, David also shows us a lack of self-control—in his disastrous encounter with Bathsheba. What does this incident teach you about the progression of sin in your own life (2 Samuel 11:1-4)?

Can you think of a recent instance where you were able (thanks to God's grace!) to stop the progression of sin and say no?

Achan failed in self-control, too. What were his progressive steps to sin (Joshua 7:21)?

Note how Joseph and Potiphar's wife (Genesis 39:7-10) show us, respectively,

...self-control–

...and a lack of self-control–

Struggling for Self-Control

These are the areas where I'm most challenged when it comes to exercising self-control. How do you struggle in these same areas?

Thoughts–

Money–

Possessions–

Addictions–

In what additional areas do you struggle?

Nurturing Self-Control

As with the other fruit, we must nurture self-control. How have the following instructions benefited you?

Begin with Christ–

Monitor your input–

Stay busy–

Say "No!"–

Pray–

> *I choose self-control...*
> I am a spiritual being.
> After this body is dead, my spirit will soar.
> I refuse to let what will rot, rule the eternal.
> I choose self-control.
> I will be impassioned only by my faith.
> I will be influenced only by God.
> I will be taught only by Christ.
> I choose self-control.[21]
> —Max Lucado

Now, my friend, may you, too, choose self-control.

13

Looking at Jesus' Applications

Begin this lesson by reading the chapter in your book, *A Woman's Walk with God*, that is titled "Looking at Jesus' Applications." Note here any new truths or challenges that stand out to you.

As we come to the end of our book about the fruit of the Spirit, we are blessed to look once again at the perfect life of our perfect Savior who perfectly lived out faithfulness, gentleness, and self-control. Let's pay close attention to the scriptures about Jesus Christ presented in this final chapter.

Begin by looking at 1 Peter 2:21. Here we learn two facts about Jesus:

First—Jesus _____ for us.

Second—Jesus left us an _____.

What does Peter say is our "calling"?

And why?

Jesus Committed No Sin

Now look at 1 Peter 2:22. Note the *first* of two facts written about Jesus' conduct and behavior:

Jesus _____.

What do these scriptures relate about the truth of this verse?
Matthew 4:23–

Matthew 26:39–

Matthew 27:4–

John 4:34–

John 5:30–

John 8:29–

John 17:4–

Acts 10:38–

2 Corinthians 5:21–

Hebrews 4:15–

Hebrews 10:9–

1 John 3:5–

As you consider your Savior and your call to follow His example and to walk "in His steps," please pause and pray about your own life. Does any glaring area of sin leap to your mind and heart? To fulfill your calling to follow Jesus, please "confess" that sin now and determine what you will do to "forsake" it (Proverbs 28:13). Purpose to implement a plan of attitude, action, and application in your life...immediately!

Jesus Spoke No Sin

Next look at 1 Peter 2:22 and note the *second* of two facts written about Jesus' conduct and behavior:

Jesus   _____.

What do these scriptures relate about the truth of this verse?

Isaiah 53:7–

Matthew 26:62-63–

Matthew 27:12-14–

Mark 14:60-61–

Mark 15:4-5–

Luke 23:9–

Once again, as you consider your Savior and your call to follow His example and to walk (and talk) "in His steps," please pause and pray about your own lips and speech habits. Does any glaring area of sin leap to your mind and heart? To fulfill your calling to follow Jesus, please "confess" that sin now and determine what you will do to "forsake" it (once again, see Proverbs 28:13). Take the time to look up these verses about godly speech...and then purpose to implement a plan of attitude, action, and application in your life...immediately!

Proverbs 10:19–

Proverbs 17:27-28–

Proverbs 19:11–

Proverbs 31:26–

Ephesians 4:29 and 31–

Colossians 3:8-9–

Colossians 4:6–

Jesus Did Not Resist

Next look at 1 Peter 2:23 and note two additional facts related about Jesus' conduct and behavior:

First–Jesus _____.

Second–Jesus _____

        but _____.

All four Gospel accounts of Jesus' crucifixion and death contain evidences of these two aspects of Jesus' conduct and behavior. But let's look specifically at Matthew's description. What do the following verses say about Jesus' treatment at the hands of His enemies during the last days of His life?

Matthew 26:67-68–

Matthew 27:26–

Matthew 27:27-32–

Matthew 27:39-40–

Matthew 27:41-43–

Matthew 27:39 and 44–

And Isaiah 53:7–

The Bible tells us that instead of sinning in act or speech, and instead of fighting back, Jesus "committed Himself" to God. What do these prayers from the lips of the suffering Savior teach us about such "committing"?

Luke 23:34–

Luke 23:46–

How can you put Jesus' practice of committing Himself in prayer to work for you the next time you suffer at the hands of another?

As you think back over all of your questions and answers thus far in this lesson on Jesus' suffering, what evidence do you see of…

…faithfulness in Jesus?

...gentleness in Jesus?

...self-control in Jesus?

> There is in the Lord Jesus a perfect evenness of various perfections. All the elements of perfect character are in lovely balance. His gentleness is never weak. His courage is never harsh. Follow Him through all the scenes of insult and outrage on that night and morning of His arrest and trial. Behold Him before Caiaphas, the High Priest, before Pilate, the governor, before Herod, the tetrarch. How His inherent greatness comes out. Not once did He lose His noble bearing or His royal dignity.[22]

Which one action or behavior of Jesus impresses you the most? And why? And is there a message here from God's Word to your heart? Please explain.

Planning for Greater Growth

 Begin this lesson by reading the chapter in your book, *A Woman's Walk with God*, that is titled "Planning for Greater Growth." Note here any new truths or challenges that stand out to you.

God's Fruit Fleshed Out

What a powerful witnessing force you and I can be when we, empowered by God's Spirit, exhibit His fruit! Judi saw Jesus in Dr. Sam's life and actions. She saw Christ's love, joy, and peace "fleshed out" in Sam's attitude toward others. Judi saw Sam acting with patience, kindness, and goodness toward those he assisted. Finally, Judi witnessed in Sam God's faithfulness, gentleness, and self-control. Who wouldn't be drawn to a person who lived out Christlikeness?!

Do you, dear one, know someone like a Dr. Sam Britten? Describe here the attitudes, actions, and applications of the nine exquisite graces that make up the fruit of the Spirit. Be specific as you detail exactly what your model of God's fruit fleshed out does...or doesn't do!

God's Word Fleshed Out in You

People were drawn to Jesus when He walked the earth because He reflected a true picture of God. Today people can be drawn to Jesus through our lives as we walk by the Spirit. Here are a few questions to assist us in our walk with God:

1. Dr. Britten "read his Bible a lot." What can you do to ensure that you set aside time for—and follow through in—reading your Bible?

2. Dr. Britten also "prayed a lot." Communing with God will always mark your life! Can you think of ways you can spend more time abiding in Christ through prayer? Be sure you make a schedule for tomorrow and for next week to get you started on a closer walk with God.

> If you and I are to abide in Christ and be women who walk with God, we must do all we can to enhance our prayer life.[23]

3. Dr. Britten's attitudes and actions and applications of godly principles moved an unbelieving observer to marvel, "This must be what Jesus was like!" Now, beloved friend, as we leave such a life-changing study, we must be sure we leave with our life changed. We must set out to spend the remainder of our days looking to God for His grace and assistance as we endeavor to cultivate His Christlike fruit.

Read again 1 John 3:2 and Dr. John Blanchard's fine words (page 209) on the purification of a believer from sin. What changes must you make...

...to purify yourself and relentlessly pursue godliness?

...to overcome sin?

...to resist temptation?

...to gain the virtues of the fruit of the Spirit?

Now for our final question: How accurately are you presenting Jesus to a watching world?

The Gospel According to You

The Gospels of Matthew, Mark, Luke and John,
Are read by more than a few,
But the one that is most read and commented on
Is the gospel according to *you*.

You are writing a gospel, a chapter each day
By things that you do and words that you say,
Men read what you write, whether faithless or true.
Say, what is the gospel according to *you*?

Do men read His truth and His love in your life,
Or has yours been too full of malice and strife?
Does your life speak of evil, or does it ring true?
Say, what is the gospel according to *you*?[24]

How to Study the Bible
—Some Practical Tips

By Jim George, Th.M.

One of the noblest pursuits a child of God can embark upon is to get to know and understand God better. The best way we can accomplish this is to look carefully at the book He has written, the Bible, which communicates who He is and His plan for mankind. There are a number of ways we can study the Bible, but one of the most effective and simple approaches to reading and understanding God's Word involves three simple steps:

Step 1: Observation—*What does the passage say?*

Step 2: Interpretation—*What does the passage mean?*

Step 3: Application—*What am I going to do about what the passage says and means?*

Observation is the first and most important step in the process. As you read the Bible text, you need to *look* carefully at what is said, and how. Look for:

• *Terms, not words.* Words can have many meanings, but terms are words used in a specific way in a specific context. (For instance, the word *trunk* could apply to a tree, a car, or a storage box. However, when you read, "That tree has a very large trunk," you know exactly what the word means, which makes it a term.)

125

- *Structure.* If you look at your Bible, you will see that the text has units called *paragraphs* (indented or marked ¶). A paragraph is a complete unit of thought. You can discover the content of the author's message by noting and understanding each paragraph unit.

- *Emphasis.* The amount of space or the number of chapters or verses devoted to a specific topic will reveal the importance of that topic (for example, note the emphasis of Romans 9–11 and Psalm 119).

- *Repetition.* This is another way an author demonstrates that something is important. One reading of 1 Corinthians 13, where the author uses the word "love" nine times in only 13 verses, communicates to us that love is the focal point of these 13 verses.

- *Relationships between ideas.* Pay close attention, for example, to certain relationships that appear in the text:

  — Cause-and-effect: "Well done, good and faithful servant; you were faithful over a few things, I will make you ruler over many things" (Matthew 25:21).

  — Ifs and thens: "If My people who are called by My name will humble themselves, and pray and seek My face, and turn from their wicked ways, then I will hear from heaven and forgive their sin and heal their land" (2 Chronicles 7:14).

  — Questions and answers: "Who is the King of glory? The Lord strong and mighty" (Psalm 24:8).

- *Comparisons and contrasts.* For example, "You have heard that it was said…but I say to you…" (Matthew 5:21).

- *Literary form.* The Bible is literature, and the three main types of literature in the Bible are discourse (the epistles), prose (Old Testament history), and poetry (the Psalms). Considering the type of literature makes a great deal of difference when you read and interpret the Scriptures.

- *Atmosphere.* The author had a particular reason or burden for writing each passage, chapter, and book. Be sure you notice the mood or tone or urgency of the writing.

After you have considered these things, you then are ready to ask the "Wh" questions:

Who?   Who are the people in this passage?

What?   What is happening in this passage?

Where?   Where is this story taking place?

When?   What time (of day, of the year, in history) is it?

Asking these four "Wh" questions can help you notice terms and identify atmosphere. The answers will also enable you to use your imagination to re-create the scene you're reading about.

As you answer the "Wh" questions and imagine the event, you'll probably come up with some questions of your own. Asking those additional questions for understanding will help to build a bridge between observation (the first step) and interpretation (the second step) of the Bible study process.

Interpretation is discovering the meaning of a passage, the author's main thought or idea. Answering the questions that arise during observation will help you in the process of interpretation. Five clues (called "the five C's") can help you determine the author's main point(s):

Context. You can answer 75 percent of your questions about a passage when you read the text. Reading the text involves looking at the near context (the verse immediately before and after) as well as the far context (the paragraph or the chapter that precedes and/or follows the passage you're studying).

Cross-references. Let Scripture interpret Scripture. That is, let other passages in the Bible shed light on the passage you are looking at. At the same time, be careful not to assume that the same word or phrase in two different passages means the same thing.

Culture. The Bible was written long ago, so when we interpret it, we need to understand it from the writers' cultural context.

Conclusion. Having answered your questions for understanding by means of context, cross-reference, and culture, you can make a preliminary statement of the passage's meaning. Remember that if your passage consists of more than one paragraph, the author may be presenting more than one thought or idea.

Consultation. Reading books known as commentaries, which are written by Bible scholars, can help you interpret Scripture.

Application is why we study the Bible. We want our lives to change; we want to be obedient to God and to grow more like Jesus Christ. After we have observed a passage and interpreted or understood it to the best of our ability, we must then apply its truth to our own life.

You'll want to ask the following questions of every passage of Scripture you study:

- How does the truth revealed here affect my relationship with God?
- How does this truth affect my relationship with others?
- How does this truth affect me?
- How does this truth affect my response to the enemy Satan?

The application step is not completed by simply answering these questions; the key is *putting into practice* what God has taught you in your study. Although at any given moment you cannot be consciously applying *everything* you're learning in Bible study, you can be consciously applying something. And when you work on applying a truth to your life, God will bless your efforts by, as noted earlier, conforming you to the image of Jesus Christ.

Helpful Bible Study Resources:

Concordance—Young's or Strong's

Bible dictionary—Unger's or Holman's

Webster's dictionary

The Zondervan Pictorial Encyclopedia of the Bible

Manners and Customs of the Bible,
James M. Freeman

Books on Bible Study:

The Joy of Discovery, Oletta Wald

Enjoy Your Bible, Irving L. Jensen

How to Read the Bible for All It's Worth, Gordon Fee &
Douglas Stuart

A Layman's Guide to Interpreting the Bible,
W. Henrichsen

Living by the Book, Howard G. Hendricks

Leading a Bible Study Discussion Group

What a privilege it is to lead a Bible study! And what joy and excitement await you as you delve into the Word of God and help others to discover its life-changing truths. If God has called you to lead a Bible study group, I know you'll be spending much time in prayer and planning and giving much thought to being an effective leader. I also know that taking the time to read through the following tips will help you to navigate the challenges of leading a Bible study discussion group and enjoying the effort and opportunity.

The Leader's Roles

As a Bible study group leader, you'll find your role changing back and forth from *expert* to *cheerleader* to *lover* to *referee* during the course of a session.

Since you're the leader, group members will look to you to be the *expert* guiding them through the material. So be well prepared. In fact, be overprepared so that you know the material better than any group member does. Start your study early in the week, and let its message simmer all week long. (You might even work several lessons ahead so that you have in mind the big picture and the overall direction of the study.) Be ready to share some additional gems that your group members wouldn't have discovered on their own. That extra insight from your study time—or that comment from a wise Bible teacher or scholar, that clever saying, that keen observation from another believer, and even an appropriate joke—adds an element of fun and keeps Bible study from becoming routine, monotonous, and dry.

Second, be ready to be the group's *cheerleader*. Your energy and enthusiasm for the task at hand can be contagious. It can also stimulate people to get more involved in their personal study as well as in the group discussion.

Third, be the *lover,* the one who shows a genuine concern for the members of the group. You're the one who will establish the atmosphere of the group. If you laugh and have fun, the group members will laugh and have fun. If you hug, they will hug. If you care, they will care. If you share, they will share. If you love, they will love. So pray every day to love the women God has placed in your group. Ask Him to show you how to love them with His love.

Finally, as the leader, you'll need to be the *referee* on occasion. That means making sure everyone has an equal opportunity to speak. That's easier to do when you operate under the assumption that every member of the group has something worthwhile to contribute. So, trusting that the Lord has taught each person during the week, act on that assumption.

Expert, cheerleader, lover, and referee—these four roles of the leader may make the task seem overwhelming. But that's not bad if it keeps you on your knees praying for your group.

A Good Start

Beginning on time, greeting people warmly, and opening in prayer gets the study off to a good start. Know what you want to have happen during your time together and make sure those things get done. That kind of order means comfort for those involved.

Establish a format and let the group members know what that format is. People appreciate being in a Bible study that focuses on the Bible. So keep the discussion on the topic and move the group through the questions. Tangents are often hard to avoid—and even harder to rein in. So be sure to focus on the answers to questions about the specific passage at hand. After all, the purpose of the group is Bible study!

Finally, as some unknown person has accurately observed, "Personal growth is one of the by-products of any effective small group. This growth is achieved when people are recognized and accepted by others. The more friendliness, mutual trust, respect, and warmth exhibited, the more likely that the member will find pleasure in the group, and, too, the more likely she will work hard toward the accomplishment of the group's goals. The effective leader will strive to reinforce desirable traits."

A Dozen Helpful Tips

Here is a list of helpful suggestions for leading a Bible study discussion group:

1. Arrive early, ready to focus fully on others and give of yourself. If you have to do any last-minute preparation, review, regrouping, or praying, do it in the car. Don't dash in, breathless, harried, late, still tweaking your plans.

2. Check out your meeting place in advance. Do you have everything you need—tables, enough chairs, a blackboard, hymnals if you plan to sing, coffee, etc.?

3. Greet each person warmly by name as she arrives. After all, you've been praying for these women all week long, so let each VIP know that you're glad she's arrived.

4. Use name tags for at least the first two or three weeks.

5. Start on time no matter what—even if only one person is there!

6. Develop a pleasant but firm opening statement. You might say, "This lesson was great! Let's get started so we can enjoy all of it!" or "Let's pray before we begin our lesson."

7. Read the questions, but don't hesitate to reword them on occasion. Rather than reading an entire paragraph of instructions, for instance, you might say, "Question 1 asks us to list some ways that Christ displayed humility. Lisa, please share one way Christ displayed humility."

8. Summarize or paraphrase the answers given. Doing so will keep the discussion focused on the topic; eliminate digressions; help avoid or clear up any misunderstandings of the text; and keep each group member aware of what the others are saying.

9. Keep moving and don't add any of your own questions to the discussion time. It's important to get through the study guide questions. So if a cut-and-dried answer is called for, you don't need to comment with anything other than a "thank you." But when the question asks for an opinion or an application (for instance, "How can this truth help us in our marriages?" or "How do *you* find time for your quiet time?"), let all who want to contribute do so.

10. Affirm each person who contributes, especially if the contribution was very personal, painful to share, or a quiet person's rare statement. Make everyone who shares a hero by saying something like, "Thank you for sharing that insight from your own life" or, "We certainly appreciate what God has taught you. Thank you for letting us in on it."

11. Watch your watch, put a clock right in front of you, or consider using a timer. Pace the discussion so that you meet your cutoff time, especially if you want time to pray. Stop at the designated time even if you haven't finished the lesson. Remember that everyone has worked through the study once; you are simply going over it again.

12. End on time. You can only make friends with your group members by ending on time or even a little early! Besides, members of your group have the next item on their agenda to attend to—picking up children from the nursery, babysitter, or school; heading home to tend to matters there; running errands; getting to bed; or spending some time with their husbands. So let them out *on time!*

Five Common Problems

In any group, you can anticipate certain problems. Here are some common ones that can arise, along with helpful solutions:

1. *The incomplete lesson*—Right from the start, establish the policy that if someone has not done the lesson, it is best for her not to answer the questions. But do try to include her responses to questions that ask for opinions or experiences. Everyone can share some thoughts in reply to a question like, "Reflect on what you know about both athletic and spiritual training and then share what you consider to be the essential elements of training oneself in godliness."

2. *The gossip*—The Bible clearly states that gossiping is wrong, so you don't want to allow it in your group. Set a high and strict standard by saying, "I am not comfortable with this conversation," or "We [not *you*] are gossiping, ladies. Let's move on."

3. *The talkative member*—Here are three scenarios and some possible solutions for each.

   a. The problem talker may be talking because she has done her homework and is excited about something she has to share. She may also know more about the subject than the others and, if you cut her off, the rest of the group may suffer.

SOLUTION: Respond with a comment like: "Sarah, you are making very valuable contributions. Let's see if we can get some reactions from the others," or "I know Sarah can answer this. She's really done her homework. How about some of the rest of you?"

b. The talkative member may be talking because she has *not* done her homework and wants to contribute, but she has no boundaries.

SOLUTION: Establish at the first meeting that those who have not done the lesson do not contribute except on opinion or application questions. You may need to repeat this guideline at the beginning of each session.

c. The talkative member may want to be heard whether or not she has anything worthwhile to contribute.

SOLUTION: After subtle reminders, be more direct, saying, "Betty, I know you would like to share your ideas, but let's give others a chance. I'll call on you later."

4. *The quiet member*—Here are two scenarios and possible solutions.

a. The quiet member wants the floor but somehow can't get the chance to share.

SOLUTION: Clear the path for the quiet member by first watching for clues that she wants to speak (moving to the edge of her seat, looking as if she wants to speak, perhaps even starting to say something) and then saying, "Just a second. I think Chris wants to say something." Then, of course, make her a hero!

b. The quiet member simply doesn't want the floor.

SOLUTION: "Chris, what answer do you have on question 2?" or "Chris, what do you think about...?" Usually after a shy person has contributed a few times, she will become more confident and more ready to share. Your role is to provide an opportunity where there is *no* risk of a wrong answer. But occasionally a group member will tell you that she would rather not be called on. Honor her request, but from time to time ask her privately if she feels ready to contribute to the group discussions.

In fact, give all your group members the right to pass. During your first meeting, explain that any time a group member does not care to share an answer, she may simply say, "I pass." You'll want to repeat this policy at the beginning of every group session.

5. *The wrong answer*—Never tell a group member that she has given a wrong answer, but at the same time never let a wrong answer go by.

SOLUTION: Either ask if someone else has a different answer or ask additional questions that will cause the right answer to emerge. As the women get closer to the right answer, say, "We're getting warmer! Keep thinking! We're almost there!"

Learning from Experience

Immediately after each Bible study session, evaluate the group discussion time. You may also want a member of your group (or an assistant or trainee or outside observer) to evaluate you periodically.

Notes

1. John MacArthur, Jr., *The MacArthur New Testament Commentary, Galatians* (Chicago: Moody Press, 1987), p. 164.

2. D. L. Moody, *Notes from My Bible and Thoughts from My Library* (Grand Rapids, MI: Baker Book House, 1979), p. 84.

3. Richard J. Foster, *Prayers from the Heart*, quoting Dame Gertrude More (San Francisco: Harper, 1994).

4. Paul Lee Tan, *Encyclopedia of 7,700 Illustrations* (Winona Lake, IN: BMH Books, 1979), p. 757.

5. D. L. Moody, *The D. L. Moody Year Book* (New York: Fleming H. Revell Company, 1900).

6. Frank S. Mead, *12,000 Religious Quotations* (Grand Rapids, MI: Baker Book House, 1989), p. 258.

7. *God's Treasury of Virtues*, quoting Jean Igelow (Tulsa, OK: Honor Books, 1995), p. 101.

8. Ibid., p. 107.

9. Herbert Lockyer, Sr., *Psalms: A Devotional Commentary* (Grand Rapids, MI: Kregel Publications, 1993), p. 119.

10. William J. Petersen and Randy Petersen, *The One Year Book of Psalms* (Wheaton, IL: Tyndale House Publishers, Inc., 1999), March 7.

11. Ralph L. Woods, *A Treasury of Contentment*, quoting Edwin Markham (New York: Trident Press, 1969).

12. Kenneth W. Osbeck, *Amazing Grace—366 Inspiring Hymn Stories for Daily Devotions* (Grand Rapids, MI: Kregel Publications,1990), p. 202.

13. Robert Van de Weyer, ed., *The Harper Collins Book of Prayers—A Treasury of Prayers Through the Ages* (San Francisco: Harper, 1993).

14. F. B. Myer, *Our Daily Walk* (Grand Rapids, MI: Zondervan Publishing House, 1972).

15. *God's Treasury of Virtues*, pp. 171-72.

16. Ibid., p. 297.

17. Osbeck, *Amazing Grace—366 Inspiring Hymn Stories for Daily Devotions*, p. 348.

18. *God's Treasury of Virtues*, p. 305.

19. Ibid, p. 372.

20. John MacArthur, Jr., *The MacArthur New Testament Commentary, Galatians*, p. 169.

21. Max Lucado, *When God Whispers Your Name* (Dallas: Word Publishing, 1994).

22. Albert M. Wells, Jr., *Inspiring Quotations—Contemporary & Classical* (Nashville: Thomas Nelson Publishers, 1988), pp. 101-02.

23. Elizabeth George, *A Woman's Walk with God* (Eugene, OR: Harvest House Publishers, 2000), p. 16.

24. Eleanor L. Doan, *The Speaker's Sourcebook* (Grand Rapids, MI: Zondervan Publishing House, 1977), p. 116.

Personal Notes

Personal Notes

_____

_____

_____

_____

_____

_____

_____

_____

_____

_____

_____

_____

_____

_____

_____

_____

_____

_____

_____

_____

About the Author

Elizabeth George is a bestselling author and speaker whose passion is to teach the Bible in a way that changes women's lives. For information about Elizabeth's books or speaking ministry, to sign up for her mailings, or to share how God has used this book in your life, please write to Elizabeth at:

Elizabeth George
P.O. Box 2879
Belfair, WA 98528

Toll-free fax/phone: 1-800-542-4611
www.elizabethgeorge.com

~

A Woman After God's Own Heart® Study Series

BIBLE STUDIES FOR BUSY WOMEN

"God wrote the Bible to change hearts and lives. Every study in this series is written with that in mind—and is specially focused on helping Christian women know how God desires for them to live."

—Elizabeth George

Sharing wisdom gleaned from more than 20 years as a women's Bible study teacher, Elizabeth has prepared insightful lessons that can be completed in 15 to 20 minutes per day. Each lesson includes thought-provoking questions and insights, Bible study tips, instructions for leading a discussion group, and a "heart response" section to make the Bible passage more personal.

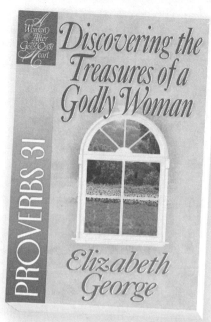

Proverbs 31 0-7369-0818-8

Philippians 0-7369-0289-9

1 Peter 0-7369-0290-2

1 Timothy 0-7369-0665-7

Judges/Ruth 0-7369-0498-0

Esther 0-7369-0489-1

James 0-7369-0490-5

Life of Mary 0-7369-0300-3

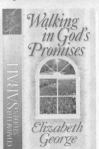

Life of Sarah 0-7369-0301-1

HARVEST HOUSE PUBLISHERS

www.harvesthousepublishers.com

Books by Elizabeth George

Beautiful in God's Eyes—The Treasures of the Proverbs 31 Woman
Powerful Promises for Every Woman
Life Management for Busy Women
Loving God with All Your Mind
A Woman After God's Own Heart®
A Woman After God's Own Heart® Deluxe Edition
A Woman After God's Own Heart® Audiobook
A Woman After God's Own Heart® Prayer Journal
A Woman's High Calling—10 Essentials for Godly Living
A Woman's Walk with God—Growing in the Fruit of the Spirit
Women Who Loved God—365 Days with the Women of the Bible
A Young Woman After God's Own Heart

Growth & Study Guides

Powerful Promises for Every Woman Growth & Study Guide
Life Management for Busy Women Growth & Study Guide
A Woman After God's Own Heart® Growth & Study Guide
A Woman's High Calling Growth & Study Guide
A Woman's Walk with God Growth & Study Guide

A Woman After God's Own Heart® Bible Study Series

Walking in God's Promises—The Life of Sarah
Cultivating a Life of Character—Judges/Ruth
Becoming a Woman of Beauty & Strength—Esther
Discovering the Treasures of a Godly Woman—Proverbs 31
Nurturing a Heart of Humility—The Life of Mary
Experiencing God's Peace—Philippians
Pursuing Godliness—1 Timothy
Growing in Wisdom & Faith—James
Putting On a Gentle & Quiet Spirit—1 Peter

Children's Books

God's Wisdom for Little Boys—Character-Building Fun from Proverbs
(co-authored with Jim George)
God's Wisdom for Little Girls—Virtues & Fun from Proverbs 31
God's Little Girl Is Helpful
God's Little Girl Is Kind